Wild Animal Babies

pictures by Carl and Mary Hauge

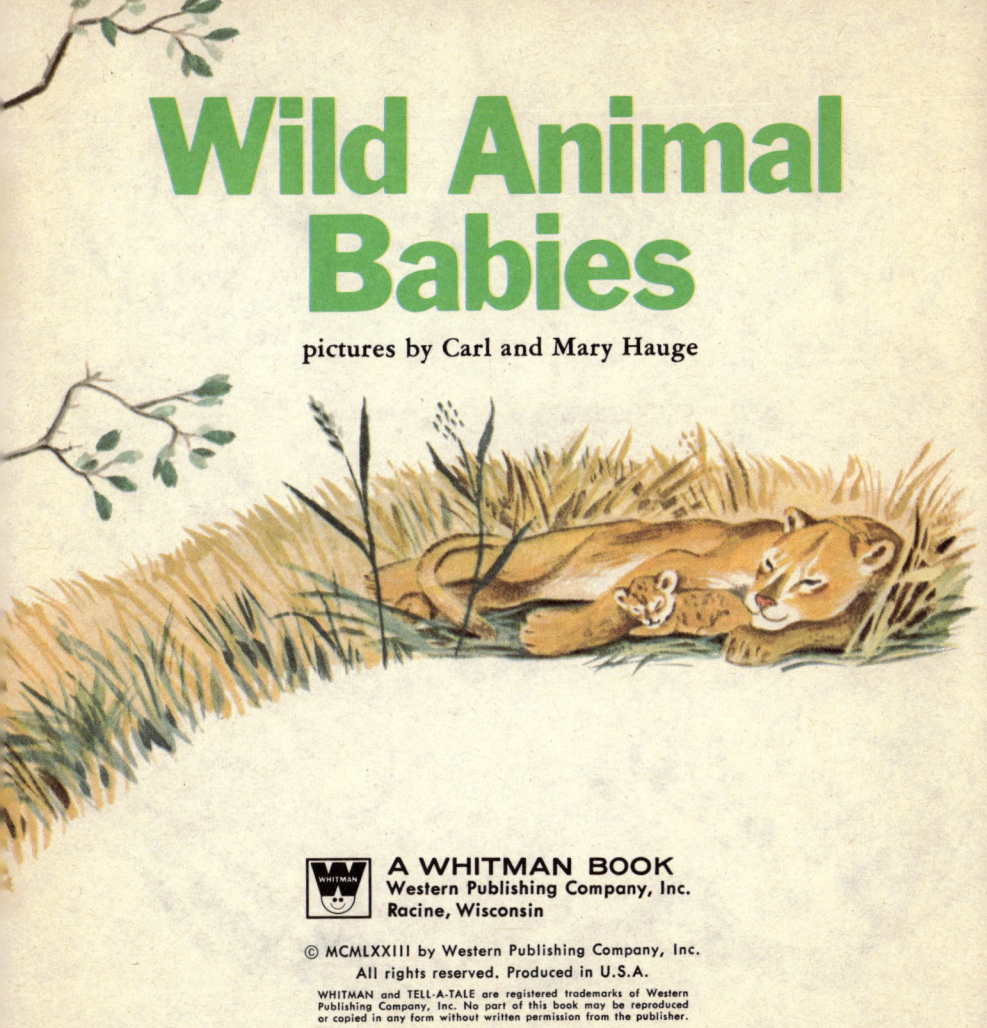

A WHITMAN BOOK
Western Publishing Company, Inc.
Racine, Wisconsin

© MCMLXXIII by Western Publishing Company, Inc.
All rights reserved. Produced in U.S.A.

WHITMAN and TELL-A-TALE are registered trademarks of Western Publishing Company, Inc. No part of this book may be reproduced or copied in any form without written permission from the publisher.

The babies play while Father LION and Mother LION watch over them.

When baby ELEPHANTS are in the water, they like to spray each other.

Very tall grass is a favorite playground for baby RHINOCEROSES.

love to eat honey and blueberries.

ZEBRAS look like black-and-white-striped horses. So do their babies.

When they grow up, these baby GIRAFFES will eat leaves from the very tallest trees.

Baby HIPPOPOTAMUS lives where it is very hot. She and her mother keep cool by standing in water.

Baby OPOSSUMS ride everywhere on their mother's back.

Baby DEER takes a drink from the stream.

Baby RACCOONS are curious.
They like to feel things.

The hot, dry desert is where Baby CAMEL lives.

Baby BISON lives on the rolling prairie.

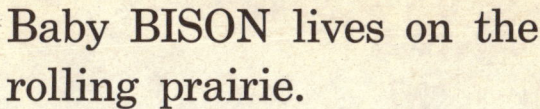

From Mother's pouch, Baby KANGAROO watches Sister play with her friend.

Baby FOXES learn to hunt by chasing grasshoppers and crickets.

Treetops are the home of these baby MONKEYS.

Mother POLAR BEAR teaches her baby how to swim.

Baby BEAVER helps her family to build a new home.

Baby SEALS love to play together in the water.

The TIGER cubs are out for a walk with their mother.

After playing and eating, baby animals like to sleep. Good night, babies.